Is anyone sick among you?

Family prayers in time of illness

Fr. Kevin J. Scallon C.M.

Jacqueline Grchan

NIHIL OBSTAT   Very Reverend José Lavastida

IMPRIMATUR   † Most Reverend Gregory M. Aymond,
Archbishop of New Orleans

Scripture quotations are from The Revised Standard Version of the Bible: Catholic Edition, copyright © 1965, 1966 the Division of Christian Education of the National Council of the Churches of Christ in the United States of America. Used by permission. All rights reserved.

DESIGN   www.lynchdesign.ie

Cover Art: The Raising of Lazarus
The painting of *The Raising of Lazarus* by Audrey Sanders depicts Martha looking at her brother Lazarus and, over her right shoulder, her grief-stricken sister Mary. The bright light in the background symbolizes the approach of Jesus, the Light of the world.

Contents

I. Introduction

Encountering Serious Illness

he illness of a loved one often brings with it fear and anxiety for the rest of the family, especially those who have to care for the sick person. They hardly know what to do when it comes to the spiritual needs of the person. If the family has lost touch with the Church, they find it hard to know what to do or how to pray. People who are seriously ill want to be put in touch with the Lord, and they need to be helped to do this. This book is intended to assist those ministering to the spiritual needs of their loved ones.

Advice for Family Members

hese days of serious illness can be a time of grace for the whole family. If possible, each one should celebrate the Sacrament of Reconciliation and attend Mass as often as possible. They ought to pray for the sick person using familiar prayers like the Rosary and the Chaplet of Divine Mercy. This is a time when old wounds can be healed and long-standing grudges forgiven. Invite everyone present to take part in these prayers. Out of respect for the sick person, no one should exclude themselves from these devotions. Everyone knows that hospitals are busy and noisy places. It is not always easy to say prayers with a sick person, but it may be possible to use some of the prayers from this book. A good time to do this is just before the end of a visit.

The Spiritual Care of the Sick

hysical care for sick people is more or less taken for granted, but spiritual care is frequently neglected. The ministry of the priest is of the greatest importance for those who are gravely ill. People sometimes use an old grudge against some long-dead priest as an excuse for not sending for the priest. Others feel embarrassed because they do not go to Church. Put all such feelings aside. Our faith is not in priests, good or bad. Our faith is in Jesus Christ, and Jesus is most perfectly present through the ministry of priests. The sooner the priest is sent for, the better. The priest will become aware if there are reasons why the sick person can not receive the sacraments. Because of his pastoral experience he will be able to deal with such matters and reconcile the person with the Church. Unfortunately, family members can neglect to call the priest, leaving their sick person without the comfort of their religion at the very time they need it the most. SEND FOR THE PRIEST AS SOON AS POSSIBLE.

Sacraments of the Sick

hrough the ministry of Reconciliation and Anointing of the Sick, the priest can bring comfort to a sick person in ways that no one else can. People need help to make their peace with God while they are still able to do so. Having listened to many such Confessions, I know the peace of soul it brings to someone who is very ill. Like Confession, the Anointing of the Sick is one of the seven sacraments or seven doors by which we may enter to find Christ. Jesus has made us His own through Baptism, Confirmation and the Eucharist. He lives in us. We become one with Him. That is what our faith teaches us. In Confession, the Sacrament of Reconciliation, Jesus forgives us when we repent, no matter what we have done. In the Sacrament of the Anointing of the Sick, we meet the healing Christ. When the priest comes he prays the prayer of Jesus, he lays his hands on the sick, and his hands become the hands of Christ. He anoints the sick person with the oil of the sick. These sacred rites make the healing Christ present and in this meeting with the soul, Jesus forgives sins and grants healing and peace.

The apostle James writes: *"Is any among you sick? Let him call for the elders of the church, and let them pray over him, anointing him with oil in the name of the Lord; and the prayer of faith will save the sick man, and the Lord will raise him up; and if he has committed sins, he will be forgiven"* (James 5:14-15).

 prinkle Holy Water around the room, and place a crucifix and a statue or picture of our Blessed Lady where they can easily be seen by the sick person.

The Miraculous Medal and the Medal of St. Benedict should be on or near the sick bed, as well as Rosary Beads and a Blessed Candle.

II. ·Prayers in the Morning

egin the prayers when the sick person has been attended to and settled for the day. If the sick person is unable to read the prayers, someone else could read them slowly, clearly and reverently.

Do not feel obliged to recite all the prayers.

The nature and degree of the illness ought always be considered.

Sign of the Cross
In the Name of the Father, and of the Son, and of the Holy Spirit.

Lord, we thank You for the beginning of this day, and we ask Your blessing upon all here present, especially *N...*

Verses from Psalm 42

*As a deer longs
for flowing streams,
so my soul longs
for you, O God.*

*My soul thirsts for God,
for the living God.
When shall I go and see
the face of God?*

*Send forth your light
and Your truth;*

*let them be my guide,
let them take me to
your holy mountain,
to the place where You reside.*

*Then will I go to
the altar of God,
to God, my gladness and delight.
I will praise you with the lyre
and harp,
O God, my God.*

Glory be to the Father, and to the Son, and to the Holy Spirit. As it was in the beginning, is now, and ever shall be, world without end.

Amen

Jesus taught us that we should pray to God as our Heavenly Father:

Our Father, Who art in Heaven,
hallowed be Thy Name.
Thy Kingdom come,
Thy will be done
on Earth as it is in Heaven.
Give us this day our daily bread,
and forgive us our trespasses
as we forgive those who trespass against us.
And lead us not into temptation,
but deliver us from evil.

Amen

*Jesus on the Cross gave us the Blessed Virgin Mary
as our Heavenly Mother:*

Hail Mary, full of grace, the Lord is with thee.
Blessed art thou among women,
and blessed is the Fruit of thy womb, Jesus.
Holy Mary, Mother of God,
pray for us sinners,
now and at the hour of our death.

Amen

The Memorare

Remember, O most gracious Virgin Mary,
that never was it known
that anyone who fled to your protection,
implored your help,
or sought your intercession was left unaided.
Inspired by this confidence,
We fly unto you,
O Virgin of virgins, our Mother;
to you do we come, before you we stand, sinful and sorrowful.
O Mother of the Word Incarnate,
despise not our petitions,
but in your mercy hear and answer us.

Amen

Let us pray to our Guardian Angel:

O Holy Guardian Angel,
gift of the Father's Love,
servant of the Eternal Word,
guiding light from the Holy Spirit
help me to worship
the most Blessed Trinity.
Friend of my soul,
walk with me the narrow path
that leads to God
and to the dwelling place of Mary.
Guard me in all my ways
that no evil may befall me.

Amen

or

Angel of God, my guardian dear,
to whom God's love commits me here,
ever this day be at my side,
to light and guard, to rule and guide.

Amen

We pray to St. Michael the Archangel to protect us from the powers of darkness:

Saint Michael the Archangel,
defend us in battle.
Be our protection against the wickedness and snares of the devil.
May God rebuke him we humbly pray,
and do thou, O Prince of the Heavenly Host,
by the power of God, cast into Hell Satan
and all the evil spirits who prowl throughout the world
seeking the ruin of souls.

Amen

An Act of Sorrow for Our Sins

O my God, I am sorry for all my sins,
for not loving others and not loving You.
Help me to live like Jesus,
and not sin again.

Amen

We offer our day to God:

Morning Offering
O Jesus, through the Immaculate Heart of Mary,
I offer You the prayers, works, joys and sufferings of this day,
for all the intentions of Your Sacred Heart,
in union with the Holy Sacrifice of the Mass
throughout the world,
in reparation for my sins,
for the needs of all my family and friends,
and in particular for the intentions of the Holy Father.

Amen

or

Prayer of Offering
by Blessed Charles de Foucauld

Father,
I abandon myself into Your hands;
do with me what You will.
Whatever You may do, I thank You:
I am ready for all; I accept all.
Let only Your Will be done in me,
and in all Your creatures.
I wish no more than this, O Lord.
Into Your hands I commend my soul.
I offer it to You with all the love of my heart,
for I love You, Lord, and so need to give myself,
to surrender myself into Your hands without reserve,
and with boundless confidence,
for You are my Father.

Amen

Prayer of One who is Unable to Receive the Sacraments

Lord, in spite of my sins and mistakes,
I know that You still love me.
I have total confidence that You can untie the knots of my life
and release me from all my troubles.
Only You can restore the wasted years.
Help me to grow in faith and bring me to eternal life.

Amen

An Act of Spiritual Communion

Lord Jesus, I hope that I will soon be able to receive You in
Holy Communion.
Until then, please come spiritually into my heart,
and renew in me the grace of my Baptism.
Give me Your peace and hope through the power of Your
Holy Spirit.

Amen

For the Sick

O God, who willed that our infirmities be borne
by Your Only Begotten Son
to show the value of human suffering,
listen in kindness to our prayers for N... who is sick.
Grant that all who are oppressed by pain,
distress or other afflictions may know
that they are chosen among those proclaimed blessed
and are united to Christ in His suffering
for the salvation of the world, through Jesus Christ, our Lord.

Amen

III. Meditations and Examination of Conscience

esus, how I have loved You,
how often I have experienced Your love.
The time has come for me to leave this place and go to You.
I look forward to that.
These days I am remembering special moments:
my First Communion, going to Lourdes,
my life and work, the young faces now old like myself.
I don't remember much of my sins,
maybe because I kept telling You about them.
You always forgave me and brought me comfort,
so I have no fear now.
Lord Jesus, You never suffered from this sickness of mine,
but You do now in my frail wasted body.
Please, Lord, join my pain to Yours on the Cross.
May it bring salvation to some poor needy soul.
Bless my family, my friends, and neighbors.
When the moment comes, allow me to receive You,
the true Bread for my journey out of this life.
Comfort me by Your Presence
in the sacraments of our Holy Church
which I have always loved.

Amen

These next meditations are intended to help those who have had difficulty in the practice of their faith.

ord, Your Name comes awkwardly to my tongue. Now I am seriously sick. The time for hollow jokes is over and Sister Death is searching for me. So here I am asking You to forgive me. I will not insult You by saying I haven't committed any sins. The truth is I have been guilty of almost every kind of sin. I have worshiped the false gods of this self-indulgent world - drink, greed and sex. All of them have abandoned me now. I seldom used Your Name except to swear or blaspheme. When I was younger I attended Mass to please my parents, but apart from that Your Word seldom echoed in my ears. Priests who came to my door I insulted and mocked. I am not proud of that now.

My marriage caused great suffering to my spouse and children. I drank the food off the table and was content to let my family fall apart. I cannot believe that I was so cruel and so selfish. My infidelities were the worst. I was truthful only when it suited me, and often trashed the reputations of many good and decent people. I never gave a penny to the poor, to the St. Vincent de Paul, the Salvation Army or anyone else. My friends of younger years went on to better things. I conveniently forgot their generosity to me on many occasions and how often they tried to help me get ahead, which in my stubborn pride I refused.

Recently I read again about the Prodigal Son. It always moves me. Lord, You gave me everything, and I have accepted nothing. I walked my own path, *I did it my way*, for all the good it has done me. Who has been praying for me that I am getting the grace to turn back to You now? Probably my mother and father who were so strong in their faith. Maybe my own family?
Not long ago a priest called to see me and offered to hear my Confession. It came as such a shock to me that I said *no*. I will *not say no* the next time.

Father, forgive this prodigal, make me good again, take away my misery and restore the wasted years. When death comes, I want to be ready. Father, I am coming home. Watch for me and have mercy. Kill the calf for me, put the cloak on my shoulders and the sandals on my feet. And don't forget the ring.

"I will arise and go to my father, and I will say to him, 'Father, I have sinned against heaven and before you; I am no longer worthy to be called your son; treat me as one of your hired servants'" (Luke 15:18-19).

Amen

The Prodigal Son

ack then, we all stopped going to Mass. Religion became something to be made fun of.

The older people were *stuck in the past,* we would say. When someone we knew died suddenly, we attended the funeral and returned to our aimless empty existence telling ourselves that *we were all okay.*

Well, Lord, I am not okay now. I am really ill and I am afraid. People call to see me. They say, "You're looking well, you know." I am not looking well, and I am not feeling well. And I am far from You.

What was that prayer we learned in school?

O my God, I am sorry for all my sins.
For not loving others, and not loving You.
Help me to live like Jesus and never sin again.

Amen

Note to caregivers:

here are many who may not be able to receive the sacraments because of certain difficulties relating to marriage, sexuality, human life, etcetera. The priest because of his pastoral experience understands this very well, and is the best person to resolve such problems. It is most important to create an atmosphere of hope for sick people, especially by prayer and by speaking of God's love

St. Anne

IV. Prayers for Various Family Members

The Prayer of a Family

"Behold, I stand at the door and knock; if any one hears my voice and opens the door, I will come in to him and eat with him, and he with me" (Revelation 3:20).

Lord Jesus, we are gathered here as a family to pray for N...
Help us with Your Holy Spirit.
We have all failed You, Lord,
each in our own way.
But You never fail us.
Take away our fears.
Give N..., whom we love,
peace and comfort in his/her final days on this earth.
Reveal yourself to him/her, Lord Jesus, and to us also.
Help us all to experience Your Divine Mercy
and the forgiveness of our sins.

Amen

Short pause for reflection

"Lord Jesus Christ, Son of God, be merciful to me, a sinner."
(Three times)

O Mary conceived without sin,
pray for us who have recourse to you.

A Prayer for a Mother

"'Can a woman forget her sucking child, that she should have no compassion on the son of her womb?' Even these may forget, yet I will not forget you" (Isaiah 49:15).

Lord Jesus, we have dreaded this day and now it has come.
It is all so unreal.
She watched us grow up and we watched her grow old.
What joy we knew with her;
Her tender love for our father.
He was the *head*, she the *heart*.
With us there was never the loud voice, or a raised hand.
Her "look at me, child" was always the last word.
I yield her to You, Lord Jesus.
You were always her Number One.

Amen

Short pause for reflection

"Lord Jesus Christ, Son of God, be merciful to me, a sinner."
(Three times)

O Mary conceived without sin,
pray for us who have recourse to you.

A Prayer for a Father

"Have I not commanded you? Be strong and of good courage; be not frightened, neither be dismayed; for the Lord your God is with you wherever you go" (Joshua 1:9).

He took me to my first game. He loved all that.
He loved his work. He helped everyone.
He loved "herself" and us, his sons and daughters.
More than anything, he loved his faith and his Church.
What wisdom he had.
I used to watch him at our family prayers,
with eyes closed, the beads dripping through his fingers.
A lesson I have never forgotten.
Loving Father, I give you back this earthly father
whom You gave me.
His work here is finished.
Our hearts will break, but in time they will mend again.

Amen

or

Lord, this is our father. Soon he will go to You.
We always loved him, but not as we love him now.
Like all of us, he did not reach his highest goals in life.
But he tried.
We know him better now and respect him more than ever.
Lord, look kindly on this good man.
We are all *prodigals* in our own way.
But he was always there for us.
Sustain him now and reward him with life everlasting.

Amen

Short Pause for reflection

A Prayer for One's Spouse

"Therefore a man leaves his father and his mother and cleaves to his wife, and they become one flesh" (Genesis 2:24).

Lord, it seems like only yesterday that we stood at the altar and exchanged our marriage vows and invited You into our family. Then we did not know how *better or worse* would be lived out in our lives. We learned that with the passing of the years, just as we learned about *sickness and health, richer and poorer.* Now we are soon to be parted, and my heart is breaking as I knew it would. Lord Jesus, You were always there with us and with our children, and You are with us still.

Lord, I commend to You this companion of our years of married life. Show Your mercy and forgiveness in the peace of a holy and happy death. In time, You will mend my heart and dry my tears until we are together again in Your Eternal Kingdom.

Amen

Pause for reflection

"Lord Jesus Christ, Son of God, be merciful to me, a sinner."
(Three times)

O Mary conceived without sin,
pray for us who have recourse to you.

A Prayer of Parents for Their Child

"Come to me, all who labor and are heavy laden, and I will give you rest. Take my yoke upon you, and learn from me; for I am gentle and lowly in heart, and you will find rest for your souls. For my yoke is easy, and my burden is light" (Matthew 11:28-30).

Father, giver of all life,
You gave us this life and now You take it back.
We can make no sense of this,
only the sense of our faith in You.
We bow before Your perfect will and plan,
and in our tears we pray, *"Thy Will be done."*

Amen

Short pause for reflection

"Lord Jesus Christ, Son of God, be merciful to me, a sinner."
(Three times)

O Mary conceived without sin,
pray for us who have recourse to you.

A Prayer for a Brother

" Martha said to Jesus, 'Lord, if you had been here, my brother would not have died. And even now I know that whatever you ask from God, God will give you.' Jesus said to her, 'Your brother will rise again.' Martha said to him, 'I know that he will rise again in the resurrection at the last day.' Jesus said to her, 'I am the resurrection and the life; he who believes in me, though he die, yet shall he live, and whoever lives and believes in me shall never die. Do you believe this?' She said to him, 'Yes, Lord; I believe that you are the Christ, the Son of God, he who is coming into the world'" (John 11:21-27).

Lord Jesus, we look at him as his life is ebbing away before our eyes.
Much of our lives we shared and enjoyed,
from childhood to manhood.
We were always close,
always glad to see each other.
Lord, look not on his sins, but on the real goodness of his heart.
Calm his fear of what lies ahead
and grant him the fullness of joy in Your Kingdom.
Comfort his family and all of us who will miss him when he is gone.

Amen

Short pause for reflection

"Lord Jesus Christ, Son of God, be merciful to me, a sinner."
(Three times)

O Mary conceived without sin,
pray for us who have recourse to you.

A Prayer for a Sister

"But the Lord answered her, 'Martha, Martha, you are anxious and troubled about many things; one thing is needful. Mary has chosen the good portion, which shall not be taken away from her'" (Luke 10:41-42).

Sisters are special people.
They have gifts which only God can give;
So it is with this good woman.
She was always third, after God and after others.
Her heart embraced her own as well as everyone else.
Her faith was unshakable
and for her, prayer could obtain anything.
Her reward awaits her.
Comfort her loved ones and all of us whom she leaves behind.
Calm her spirit, Lord, relieve her pain,
and grant her a peaceful passing from this life.
Amen

Short pause for reflection

"Lord Jesus Christ, Son of God, be merciful to me, a sinner."
(Three times)

O Mary conceived without sin,
pray for us who have recourse to you.

Prayer of One Caring for the Sick

"Then the righteous will answer him, 'Lord, when did we see thee hungry and feed thee, or thirsty and give thee drink? And when did we see thee a stranger and welcome thee, or naked and clothe thee? And when did we see thee sick or in prison and visit thee?' And the King will answer them, 'Truly, I say to you, as you did it to one of the least of these my brethren, you did it to me'" (Matthew 25:37-40).

Lord Jesus, I never imagined that I could do this.
Only Your grace has made it possible.
Help me to realize that it is You Whom I am caring for,
that it is Your Body that I am washing and feeding.
Give me eyes to see You and give me patience and
strength when I need it.

Amen

Short pause for reflection

"Lord Jesus Christ, Son of God, be merciful to me, a sinner."
(Three times)

O Mary conceived without sin,
pray for us who have recourse to you.

V. Prayers in the Evening

 he traditional recitation of the Rosary or the Chaplet of Divine Mercy as the final prayer of the day can create an atmosphere of peace, both for the family and for the sick person. It should be recited softly and with reverence.

Sign of the Cross
In the Name of the Father, and of the Son, and of the Holy Spirit.

Let us ask pardon for the failures of this day:

Act of Contrition

My Father, I have sinned against You,
I have offended You Who have been so good to me.
Father, help me by Your grace
to change my life and turn away from sin.

Amen

Psalm 134

Come, bless the Lord,
all you servants of the Lord,
who minister by night in the house of the Lord,
in the courts of the house of our God.

Raise your hands to the sanctuary and bless the Lord.
May the Lord bless you from Zion,
he who made heaven and earth.

Glory be to the Father, and to the Son, and to the Holy Spirit. As it was in the beginning, is now, and ever shall be, world without end.

Amen

or

Psalm 130

Out of the depths I cry to you, O Lord,
O Lord, hear my voice!
Let your ears pay attention
to the voice of my supplication.

If you should mark our evil,
O Lord, who would stand?
But with you is forgiveness,
and for that you are revered.

I waited for the Lord, my soul waits,
and I put my hope in his word.
My soul expects the Lord
more than watchmen the dawn.

O Israel, hope in the Lord,
for with him is unfailing love
and with him full deliverance.
He will deliver Israel
from all its sins.

Glory be to the Father, and to the Son, and to the Holy Spirit. As it was in the beginning, is now, and ever shall be, world without end.

Amen

Deuteronomy 6:4-7

Hear, O Israel:
The Lord our God is one Lord;
and you shall love the Lord your God
with all your heart,
and with all your soul,
and with all your might.
And these words which I command you this day
shall be upon your heart;
and you shall teach them diligently to your children,
and shall talk of them when you sit in your house,
and when you walk by the way,
and when you lie down,
and when you rise.

or

Ephesians 4:26-27

Be angry but do not sin: do not let the sun go down on your anger, and
give no opportunity to the devil.

or

Matthew 11:28-29

Come to me, all who labor and are heavy laden, and I will give you
rest. Take my yoke upon you, and learn from me; for I am gentle and
lowly in heart, and you will find rest for your souls.

Into Your hands, Lord, I commend my spirit.
Into Your hands, Lord, I commend my spirit.
Into Your hands, Lord, I commend my spirit.

Canticle of Simeon

Save us, Lord, while we are awake; protect us while we sleep; that we may keep watch with Christ and rest with Him in peace.

At last, all-powerful Master, You give leave to Your servant to go in peace, according to Your promise.
For my eyes have seen Your salvation
which You have prepared for all nations,
the Light to enlighten the Gentiles
and give glory to Israel, Your people.
Glory to the Father, and to the Son,
and to the Holy Spirit,
as it was in the beginning, is now,
and will be for ever.

Save us, Lord, while we are awake; protect us while we sleep; that we may keep watch with Christ and rest with Him in peace.

Amen

A Final Prayer
(A beautiful prayer of John Henry Cardinal Newman, the great English convert and theologian. He was beatified by Pope Benedict XVI on his visit to England in 2010.)

O Lord, support us all the day long of this troublous life,
until the shadows lengthen and evening comes,
and the busy world is hushed,
and the fever of life is over,
and our work is done.
Then, in Your mercy,
grant us a safe lodging and a holy rest
and peace at the last.

Amen

Hail Holy Queen

Hail, holy Queen, Mother of Mercy,
Our life, our sweetness and our hope.
To thee do we cry, poor banished children of Eve.
To thee to we send up our sighs,
mourning and weeping in this valley of tears.
Turn, then, most gracious advocate,
thine eyes of mercy toward us,
and after this, our exile,
show unto us the Blessed Fruit of thy womb, Jesus.
O clement, O loving, O sweet Virgin Mary.

V. Pray for us, O holy Mother of God.

R. That we may be made worthy of the promises of Christ.

"*Lord Jesus Christ, Son of God, Be merciful to me, a sinner.*"
(*Three times*)

O Mary conceived without sin,
pray for us who have recourse to you.

VI. The Holy Rosary

To say that the Rosary is long and repetitious is to completely misunderstand this beautiful prayer. The Church East and West, and other religions, repeat short prayers as a means of creating an atmosphere of quiet contemplation. Saint John Paul II commented that *"The Rosary is my favourite prayer. A marvelous prayer! Marvelous in its simplicity and its depth... Against the background of the words Hail Mary, the principal events of the life of Jesus Christ pass before the eyes of the soul. They take shape in the complete series of the ... mysteries, and they put us in living communion with Jesus through – we might say – the heart of His Mother. At the same time our heart can embrace in the decades of the Rosary all the events that make up the lives of individuals, families, nations, the Church, and all mankind... Thus the simple prayer of the Rosary marks the rhythm of human life."*

Saint John Paul II, Angelus Message, October 29, 1978

Opening Prayer:

O Lord, open my lips.
And my tongue shall announce thy praise.
Incline unto my aid, O Lord.
O Lord, make haste to help me.

Amen

Apostles Creed:

I believe in God, the Father Almighty,
Creator of Heaven and Earth;
and in Jesus Christ, His only Son our Lord,
Who was conceived by the Holy Spirit,
born of the Virgin Mary,
suffered under Pontius Pilate,
was crucified, died, and was buried.
He descended into Hell.
The third day He rose again from the dead.
He ascended into Heaven,
and sits at the right hand of God, the Father almighty;
from there He shall come to judge the living and the dead.
I believe in the Holy Spirit, the holy Catholic Church,
the communion of saints, the forgiveness of sins,
the resurrection of the body and life everlasting.

Amen.

Then pray: 1 Our Father, 3 Hail Marys (for the virtues of Faith, Hope and Charity) and 1 Glory Be:

Our Father, Who art in Heaven,
hallowed be Thy Name.
Thy Kingdom come,
Thy will be done
on Earth as it is in Heaven.
Give us this day our daily bread,
and forgive us our trespasses
as we forgive those who trespass against us.
And lead us not into temptation,
but deliver us from evil.

Amen

Hail Mary, full of grace, the Lord is with thee.
Blessed art thou among women,
and blessed is the Fruit of thy womb, Jesus.

Holy Mary, Mother of God,
pray for us sinners,
now and at the hour of our death.

Amen

Glory be to the Father, and to the Son,
and to the Holy Spirit.
As it was in the beginning, is now,
and ever shall be, world without end.

Amen

Fatima Prayer

O my Jesus,
forgive us our sins,
save us from the fires of Hell.
Lead all souls to Heaven,
especially those in most need of Thy mercy.

Amen

While meditating on each of the Mysteries, recite:
one Our Father (large beads), ten Hail Marys (small beads) and one
Glory Be (before the next large bead) followed by the Fatima Prayer to
pray a complete decade of the Rosary.

The Joyful Mysteries
(Recite Mondays and Saturdays, and Sundays during Advent)
1   The Annunciation (Lk 1:26-38)
2   The Visitation of Mary to Elizabeth (Lk 1:39 47)
3   The Nativity of our Lord Jesus Christ (Lk 2:1-7)
4   The Presentation of Jesus in the Temple (Lk 2:22- 32)
5   The finding of Jesus in the Temple (Lk 2:41-52)

The Luminous Mysteries
(Recite Thursdays)
1   The Baptism of Jesus in the Jordan (Mt 3:113-17)
2   The Wedding Feast at Cana (Jn 2:1-11)
3   The Proclamation of the Kingdom (Lk 4:14-21)
4   The Transfiguration (Mk 9:2-8)
5   The Institution of the Eucharist (Lk 22:14-20)

The Sorrowful Mysteries
(Recite Tuesdays and Fridays, also Sundays during Lent):
1   The Agony in the Garden (Mk 14:32-36)
2   The Scourging at the Pillar (Jn 18:28-38;19:1)
3   The Crowning with Thorns (Mk 15:16-20)
4   The Carrying of the Cross (Jn 19:l2-16)
5   The Crucifixion of Jesus (Lk 23:33-34; 39-46)

The Glorious Mysteries
(Recite Sundays and Wednesdays, also Sundays from Easter until Advent)
1   The Resurrection of Jesus (Lk 24:1-8)
2   The Ascension of Jesus into Heaven (Lk 24:50-53)
3   The Descent of the Holy Spirit (Jn 20:19-23)
4   The Assumption of Mary into Heaven
5   The Coronation of Our Lady in Heaven

Hail Holy Queen

Hail, holy Queen, Mother of Mercy,
Our life, our sweetness and our hope.
To thee do we cry, poor banished children of Eve.
To thee to we send up our sighs,
mourning and weeping in this valley of tears.
Turn, then, most gracious advocate,
thine eyes of mercy toward us,
and after this, our exile,
show unto us the Blessed Fruit of thy womb, Jesus.
O clement, O loving, O sweet Virgin Mary.

V. Pray for us, O holy Mother of God.
R. That we may be made worthy of the promises of Christ.

Prayer After the Rosary

O God, Whose only-begotten Son,
by His life, death and Resurrection,
has purchased for us the rewards of eternal life.
Grant, we beseech Thee, that while meditating
upon these mysteries of the Most Holy Rosary
of the Blessed Virgin Mary,
we may imitate what they contain
and obtain what they promise,
through the same Christ our Lord.

Amen

May the Divine Assistance remain always with us and may the
souls of the faithful departed, through the mercy of God, rest
in peace.

Amen

Music

 uch has been written about the power of music to touch and console the human spirit, especially of people who are ill. Do not hesitate to play recordings of classical or sacred music, or familiar hymns. There are also recordings of the Rosary and the Chaplet of Divine Mercy. Playing these in the presence of the sick can create an atmosphere of prayer and peace, and bring great comfort and grace to all.

VII. The Chaplet of Divine Mercy

he Chaplet of Divine Mercy is a relatively recent devotion revealed by Christ to St. Faustina. This Chaplet is prayed on rosary beads. It has come to be much loved by people everywhere. Read what Jesus said of it:

"Say unceasingly this chaplet that I have taught you. Anyone who says it will receive great Mercy at the hour of death. Priests will recommend it to sinners as the last hope. Even the most hardened sinner, if he recites this Chaplet even once, will receive grace from My Infinite Mercy. I want the whole world to know My Infinite Mercy. I want to give unimaginable graces to those who trust in My Mercy..." (Diary, 687).

"....When they say this Chaplet in the presence of the dying, I will stand between My Father and the dying person not as the just judge but as the Merciful Saviour" (Diary, 1541).

Sign of the Cross
In the Name of the Father, and of the Son, and of the Holy Spirit.

Opening Prayers:

You expired, Jesus, but the source of life gushed forth for souls, and the ocean of Mercy opened up for the whole world. O Fount of Life, unfathomable Divine Mercy, envelop the whole world and empty Yourself out upon us.

O Blood and Water, which gushed forth from the Heart of Jesus as a fountain of Mercy for us, I trust in You!

1. Using Rosary beads begin by prayering:

One Our Father, one Hail Mary and the Apostles Creed.

2. Then on the Our Father beads say the following:

Eternal Father, I offer You the Body and Blood, Soul and Divinity of Your Dearly Beloved Son, our Lord Jesus Christ, in atonement for our sins and those of the whole world.

3. On the 10 Hail Mary beads say the following:

For the sake of His Sorrowful Passion, have Mercy on us and on the whole world.

(Repeat step 2 and 3 for all five decades).

4. Conclude with (three times):

Holy God, Holy Mighty One, Holy Immortal One, have Mercy on us and on the whole world.

Closing Prayer:

Eternal God, in Whom Mercy is endless and the treasury of compassion inexhaustible, look kindly upon us and increase Your Mercy in us, that in difficult moments we might not despair nor become despondent, but with great confidence submit ourselves to Your Holy Will, which is Love and Mercy itself.

VIII. Prayers as Life Draws to a Close

hese prayers are offered for the sick person. They should be prayed in a quiet time when the sick person might be able to listen.

We read in the Gospel of John

[Jesus visits the home of Martha and Mary, having learned that Lazarus their brother had died.]

"When Martha heard that Jesus was coming, she went and met him, while Mary sat in the house. Martha said to Jesus, 'Lord, if you had been here, my brother would not have died. And even now I know that whatever you ask from God, God will give you.' Jesus said to her, 'Your brother will rise again.' Martha said to him, 'I know that he will rise again in the resurrection at the last day.' Jesus said to her, 'I am the resurrection and the life; he who believes in me, though he die, yet shall he live, and whoever lives and believes in me shall never die. Do you believe this?' She said to him, 'Yes, Lord; I believe that you are the Christ, the Son of God, he who is coming into the world'" (John 11:20-27).

Short pause for reflection

Act of Faith

O my God, I firmly believe that You are one God
in three Divine Persons,
Father, Son and Holy Spirit.
I believe that Your Divine Son became flesh, died for our sins,
and that He will come to judge the living and the dead.
I believe these and all that the Holy Catholic Church teaches.

Amen

Act of Hope

O my God, relying on Your almighty power,
Your infinite mercy and Your promises,
I hope to obtain pardon for my sins, the help of Your grace,
and life everlasting through the merits of Jesus Christ,
my Lord and Redeemer.

Amen

Act of Love

O my God, I love You above all things,
with my whole heart and soul,
because You are all good and worthy of my love.
I love my neighbor as myself for love of You.
I forgive all who have wronged me
and ask pardon of all whom I have injured.

Amen

We pray for the protection of St. Michael the Archangel:

Saint Michael the Archangel,
defend us in battle.
Be our protection against the wickedness
and snares of the devil.
May God rebuke him we humbly pray,
and do thou, O Prince of the Heavenly Host,
by the power of God, cast into Hell Satan
and all evil spirits who prowl throughout the world
seeking the ruin of souls.

Amen

Prayer for the Grace of a Happy Death

O Most Merciful Father,
hear the prayers we offer for those who will die this day.
They have been redeemed by the Precious Blood of Jesus Your Son.
May they leave this world without stain of sin
and find eternal rest in the embrace of Your Mercy,
through Christ, our Lord.

Amen

Prayer to St. Joseph

Jesus, Mary and Joseph, I give you my heart and soul.
Jesus, Mary and Joseph, assist me in my last agony.
Jesus, Mary and Joseph, may I breathe out my soul in peace with you.

Amen

Intercessions to the Holy Trinity

Loving Father, deliver *N*...

- as You delivered Abraham *Hear us, O Lord*
- as You delivered Job from his trials *Hear us, O Lord*
- as You delivered Moses and the chosen
  people from Egypt *Hear us, O Lord*
- as You delivered Daniel from the lion's den *Hear us, O Lord*
- as You delivered David from Goliath *Hear us, O Lord*
- as You delivered Peter and Paul from prison *Hear us, O Lord*

Lord Jesus, comfort *N*...

- as You comforted St. Joseph by
  the grace of a happy death *Have mercy, O Lord*
- as You comforted Martha and Mary
  by raising Lazarus from the dead *Have mercy, O Lord*
- as You comforted the Widow of Nain
  by bringing her son back to life *Have mercy, O Lord*
- as You comforted the Good Thief
  on the Cross *Have mercy, O Lord*
- as You comforted the Apostles
  in the Upper Room *Have mercy, O Lord*

Holy Spirit ...

- strengthen us all with the Good News
  of the Risen Christ *Come, Holy Spirit*
- strengthen *N*... with the consolation
  of Your presence *Come, Holy Spirit*
- strengthen *N*... with protection against
  the powers of darkness *Come, Holy Spirit*
- strengthen *N*... with forgiveness and
  perseverance at the moment of death *Come, Holy Spirit*

Let us pray:

Lord Jesus, we entrust N... to You who died for us.
Come with Your Mother Mary,
with the angels and saints to take him/her home.
May your death bring him/her forgiveness and peace.
May he/she march into Heaven
under the banner of Your Holy Cross
and see You face to face forever.

Amen

 plenary indulgence is the application by the Church of the infinite merits of Christ's death and resurrection in order to obtain the complete remission of all temporal punishment due to our sins. We ought to immediately express our deepest gratitude to Almighty God for this wonderful gift of His Mercy.

Prayer to Obtain Plenary Indulgence

O Lord, my God, with my whole heart I willingly accept
whatever kind of death
You will send to me,
with all its anxieties, pains and sufferings.

Amen

Indulgence granted by Pope Pius X, 9 March 1904

Prayer at the Moment of Death

In the Name of God, the Almighty Father, Who created you,
in the Name of Jesus Christ, Son of the Living God,
Who suffered for you,
in the Name of the Holy Spirit, Who was poured out upon you,
go forth, faithful Christian.
May you live in peace this day.
May your home be with God in Heaven,
with Mary, the Virgin Mother of God,
with St. Joseph, and all the angels and saints.

Amen

Prayer of the Bereaved

Lord, it is over now;
we somehow managed with Your help to get through it all.
Thank You, Lord Jesus.
We never knew that death could be so beautiful, so peaceful.
There were many graces, not least for us who are left behind.
There was a sense of joy in it all, like a kind of spiritual retreat.

Lord, continue to heal us who remain.
Cleanse our broken hearts with the healing tears of grief.
Life must go on until that day comes for each of us.
Let the love we have experienced during these days
grow in all of us.

Mother Mary, thank you for your prayerful, loving presence,
and for allowing us to stand with you by the Cross of your Son.

Amen

here is a custom of holding a lighted blessed candle in the hand of the dying person. The candle symbolizes the presence of the Risen Christ. Holy water should be sprinkled around the room. These sacramentals have great power to ward off the temptations and attacks of the evil one.

IX. Additional Prayers

Litany of the Holy Name of Jesus

Lord, have mercy on us.	*Christ, have mercy on us.*
Lord, have mercy on us. Jesus, hear us.	*Jesus, graciously hear us.*
God the Father of Heaven	*Have mercy on us.*
God the Son, Redeemer of the world,	"
God the Holy Spirit,	"
Holy Trinity, one God,	"
Jesus, Son of the living God,	*Have mercy on us.*
Jesus, splendor of the Father,	"
Jesus, brightness of eternal light,	"
Jesus, king of glory,	"
Jesus, sun of justice,	"
Jesus, Son of the Virgin Mary,	"
Jesus, most amiable,	"
Jesus, most admirable,	"
Jesus, the mighty God,	"
Jesus, Father of the world to come,	"
Jesus, angel of great counsel,	"
Jesus, most powerful,	"
Jesus, most patient,	"
Jesus, most obedient,	"
Jesus, meek and humble of heart,	"
Jesus, lover of chastity,	"
Jesus, lover of us,	"
Jesus, God of peace,	"
Jesus, author of life,	"
Jesus, example of virtues,	"
Jesus, zealous lover of souls,	"
Jesus, our God,	"
Jesus, our refuge,	"

Jesus, father of the poor,   *Have mercy on us.*
Jesus, treasure of the faithful,   "
Jesus, good shepherd,   "
Jesus, true light,   "
Jesus, eternal wisdom,   "
Jesus, infinite goodness,   "
Jesus, our way and our life,   "
Jesus, joy of angels,   "
Jesus, king of the patriarchs,   "
Jesus, master of the apostles,   "
Jesus, teacher of the evangelists,   "
Jesus, strength of martyrs,   "
Jesus, light of confessors,   "
Jesus, purity of virgins,   "
Jesus, crown of saints,   "
Be merciful,   *Spare us, O Jesus.*
Be merciful,   *Graciously hear us, O Jesus.*
From all evil,   *Deliver us, O Jesus.*
From all sin,   "
From Your wrath,   "
From the snares of the devil,   "
From the spirit of fornication,   "
From everlasting death,   "
From the neglect of Your inspirations,   "
By the mystery of Your holy Incarnation   "
By Your nativity,   "
By Your infancy,   "
By Your most divine life,   "
By Your labors,   "
By Your agony and passion,   "
By Your Cross and dereliction,   "
By Your sufferings,   "
By Your death and burial,   "
By Your resurrection,   "
By Your ascension,   "
By Your institution of the most Holy Eucharist,   "
By Your joys,   "
By Your glory,   "

Lamb of God, who takes away the sins of the world,
Spare us, O Jesus.

Lamb of God, who takes away the sins of the world,
Graciously hear us, O Jesus.

Lamb of God, who takes away the sins of the world,
Have mercy on us, O Jesus.

Jesus, hear us.
Jesus, graciously hear us.

Let us pray:

O Lord Jesus Christ, You have said, *"Ask and you shall receive, seek and you shall find, knock and it shall be opened to you."* Grant, we beg of You, to us who ask it, the gift of Your most Divine Love, that we may ever love You with our whole heart, in word and deed, and never cease praising You.

Amen

Litany of the Blessed Virgin Mary

Lord, have mercy.	*Christ have mercy.*
Lord, have mercy. Christ hear us.	*Christ graciously hear us.*

God the Father of Heaven,	*Have mercy on us.*
God the Son, Redeemer of the world,	*"*
God the Holy Spirit,	*"*
Holy Trinity, one God,	*"*

Holy Mary,   *Pray for us.*
Holy Mother of God,   "
Holy virgin of virgins,   "
Mother of Christ,   "
Mother of divine grace,   "
Mother most pure,   "
Mother most chaste,   "
Mother inviolate,   "
Mother undefiled,   "
Mother most amiable,   "
Mother most admirable,   "
Mother of good counsel,   "
Mother of our Creator,   "
Mother of our Saviour,   "
Virgin most prudent,   "
Virgin most venerable,   "
Virgin most powerful,   "
Virgin most merciful,   "
Virgin most faithful,   "
Mirror of justice,   "
Seat of wisdom,   "
Cause of our joy,   "
Spiritual vessel,   "
Vessel of honor,   "
Singular vessel of devotion,   "
Mystical rose,   "
Tower of David,   "
Tower of ivory,   "
House of gold,   "
Ark of the covenant,   "
Gate of Heaven,   "
Morning star,   "
Health of the sick,   "
Refuge of sinners,   "
Comforter of the afflicted,   "

Help of Christians,	*Pray for us.*
Queen of angels,	"
Queen of patriarchs,	"
Queen of prophets,	"
Queen of apostles,	"
Queen of martyrs,	"
Queen of confessors,	"
Queen of virgins,	"
Queen of all saints,	"
Queen conceived without original sin,	"
Queen assumed into heaven,	"
Queen of the most holy Rosary,	"
Queen of families,	"
Queen of peace,	"

Lamb of God, who takes away the sins of the world,
Spare us, O Lord.

Lamb of God, who takes away the sins of the world,
Graciously hear us, O Lord.

Lamb of God, who takes away the sins of the world,
Have mercy on us.

Pray for us, O holy Mother of God.
That we may be made worthy of the promises of Christ.

Let us pray:

Grant, we beseech You, O Lord God, that we Your servants may enjoy perpetual health of mind and body, and by the glorious intercession of Blessed Mary, ever Virgin, may we be freed from present sorrow, and rejoice in eternal happiness. Through Christ our Lord.

Amen

St. Patrick's Breastplate

he *"Lorica"* or protective armour of a warrior inspires this name. This prayer was written around the year 850 A.D. and at that time was believed by some to have been composed by St. Patrick himself three centuries previously. Even if not written by him it expresses his spirituality as revealed in his *"Confession."*

It provides a framework for our own prayer, containing all that pertains to the heart of our faith - belief in the worship of the Holy Trinity, in the Incarnation of Christ and His work for our salvation, the co-workers of Christ in His Church, the Presence of God in all His creation and His guidance and help in all our needs against all the powers of evil. It then calls on Christ's special protection, and prays that we be immersed in Christ Who has promised to come and live in us.

Finally, it returns to the Holy Trinity again, the Bedrock of our Faith. It is a prayer that should be better known, and more often used.

I arise today   *The Holy Trinity*
Through a mighty strength, the invocation of the Trinity,
Through belief in the Threeness
Through confession of the Oneness
Of the Creator of Creation.

I arise today   *Christ*
Through the strength of Christ's birth with His Baptism,
Through the strength of His Crucifixion with His burial,
Through the strength of His Resurrection with His Ascension,
Through the strength of his descent for the judgment of
doom.

I arise today   *Angels, saints, prophets, apostles*
Through the strength of the love of the cherubim,
In the obedience of the angels,
In the service of the archangels,
In the hope of the resurrection to meet with reward,
In the prayers of the patriarchs,
In prediction of prophets,
In preaching of apostles,
In faith of confessors,
In innocence of holy virgins,
In deeds of righteous men.

I arise today   *God present in everything*
Through the strength of Heaven,
Light of sun, radiance of moon,
Splendor of fire,
Speed of lightening,
Swiftness of winds,
Depth of sea,
Stability of earth,
Firmness of rock.

I arise today   *God's guidance and help in every need*
    Through God's strength to pilot me,
    God's might to uphold me,
    God's wisdom to guide me,
    God's eye to look before me,
    God's ear to hear me,
    God's word to speak to me,
    God's hand to guard me,
    God's way to lie before me,
    God's shield to protect me,
    God's host to save me,
    From snares of devils,
    From temptations of vices,
    From everyone who shall wish me ill,
    Afar and anear,
    Alone and in a multitude.

I summon today   *Against all the powers of evil*
all these powers between me and those evils
    Against every cruel merciless power
        that may oppose my body and soul,
    Against incarnations of false prophets,
    Against black laws of pagandom,
    Against false laws of heresies,
    Against craft of idolatry,
    Against spells of witches and smiths and wizards,
    Against every knowledge
        that corrupts man's body and soul.

Christ to shield me today *Christ's protection*
  Against poisoning, against burning,
  Against drowning, against wounding,
  So there may come to me an abundance of reward.

Christ with me, Christ before me *Immersion in Christ*
  Christ behind me, Christ in me,
  Christ beneath me, Christ above me,
  Christ on my right, Christ on my left,
  Christ when I lie down, Christ when I sit down,
  Christ when I arise,
  Christ in the heart of every one who thinks of me,
  Christ in the mouth of every one who speaks of me,
  Christ in the eye of every one that sees me,
  Christ in every ear that hears me.

I arise today *The Trinity*
  Through a mighty strength, the invocation of the Trinity,
  Through belief in the Threeness,
  Through confession of the Oneness of the Creator
    of Creation.

Curtha ar fáil ag Cumann na Sagart

Fr. Kevin Scallon, CM is a Vincentian priest. He has experienced many facets of the priestly ministry, mostly in ministering to priests in many countries around the world with Sr. Briege McKenna, OSC. He is the author of the book *"I Will Come Myself."*

Mrs. Jacqueline Grchan has been personal assistant to Fr. Kevin Scallon, CM and Sr. Briege McKenna, OSC for many years. She is married to Joseph Grchan and they have eight children and one grand-child. Her work for the church in these combined ministries of Fr. Kevin and Sr. Briege has in every way been exceptional.

Is anyone sick among you?

Is anyone sick among you?

45983021R00038